Greek Mythology

Tales from the Greek Pantheon

Adam Andino

Table of Contents

Introduction

Imagine living in ancient times and having to make sense of the world. It seems like everything is out to kill you and you have no clue why. The solution, of course, is to tell a story about it. This was what ancient Greeks did; in a way that was so beautiful and intricate, it still captures our minds today. What is known today as mythology was to them their religion and the very basis of their society. Tellers of these stories were considered blessed by the Muses. The tales they spun were the whispering of the Muses about the god's adventures. Each tale provided guidance and insight into what was taking place on the top of Mount Olympus. They were a source of inspiration and instruction, and provided hope, despair, warnings, explanations, and yes, even entertainment.

The stories from Ancient Greece were representations of multiple aspects of humanity and their perception of the world. The gods were not perfect beings: they loved, hated, and acted as humans would. They were divine mirrors of human desires. Greek mythology centered on twelve major gods, with each god representing an aspect of nature. There were gods of thunder, water, death, life, fertility, and many more. Outside of the twelve Olympians, the Greeks believed in and worshiped scores of other gods. Their philosophers (Plato, Socrates, Aristotle...) stand as proof of their desire to explore and explain natural phenomena. As a result of this desire to be one with and understand their environment, dozens of gods and spirits sprang from their imaginations. Much of these stories were oral, though later Greeks tried to capture them in written form. It is interesting to note that there were those in Greek society who considered the stories to be exaggerated entertainment. However, the vast majority incorporated the tales into their daily lives and spiritual beliefs. It was believed that holding atheistic or agnostic views was sacrilege, and the unbeliever would be severely punished by the gods.

Religion was a deeply personal and daily activity in Ancient Greece. Church and state were one and the same. All aspects of life were influenced by the gods, who regularly intervened in human life. They believed the gods loved, demanded, and responded to worship. As a result, they built temples and sacred sites, sacrificed animals, and gave libations (this is the pouring out of a drink, usually some form of alcohol, as an offering to their gods). Festivals, artistic competitions, and sporting events were used to honor the gods and evoke their favors. During these events, war was prohibited, and safe passage was granted to all. Many cities had patron gods. For example, Athena was the patron god of Athens and Apollo the patron of Delphi. Some places were believed to have a deep spiritual connection to the gods. As a result, these places were visited by royalty and peasants alike. Their priests were held in high esteem and a trip to these areas was considered a pilgrimage.

The gods were believed to have representatives in the form of priests, Oracles, and attendants. The Greeks sought these representatives out to perform rites and bestow the wisdom and command of the gods. The Greeks believed the future could be seen through the use of augury. The entrails of animals who had been sacrificed- such as pigs, goats, sheep and cows- were often examined to ascertain upcoming events. The sex of the animals was always the same as the god being called upon or honored. It is interesting to note that, despite the limited role of women in Greek society, they could be priests as well. However, their selection was dependent on their virginity, and if they had passed menopause. While the priests performed the ceremonies, theological discourse on the gods was the purview of city officials.

While many engaged in public, formal worship, personal worship was just as important to the ancient Greeks. The floor of the fireplace—called the hearth—was considered sacred and persons would offer gifts, incense, wine, flowers, and food to honor their chosen god. Those who had the means performed their own animal sacrifices at personal sites. It was believed the commands of the gods could be found in regular conversation and the behavior of animals. Whole groups had rites that were known only to them, and it was believed that performing these rites would bestow special gifts on the performers. Rites were practiced on a variety of occasions, such as before and during war, when setting off on a journey, at marriages, and at coming-of-age events, to name a few.

Religion was an intricate part of Ancient Greek society. It was reflected in their daily actions as they sought to honor and seek the aid of their many gods- particularly the twelve main gods of Mount Olympus. The stories of these gods became a guide to Ancient Greeks and a source of fascination and entertainment to modern society.

Chapter 1: The Gods of Olympus

The twelve major gods of the Greek pantheon were at the center of Greek mythology. These gods were believed to reside on the tallest mountain in Greece: Mount Olympus. Stories are told of their rise to power and their relationships with mortals and monsters. The gods blessed, cursed, and created. They were capricious and displayed the same desires and emotions as mankind.

Although most stories only refer to there being 12 Olympian gods, this chapter lists 14. Hades is the 13th god included in this list despite not actually being an considered an Olympian. Rather than living atop Mount Olympus, Hades resides in the Underworld, of which is he the ruler. And the reasoning for there being a 14th god listed here is because depending upon which source you refer to, some stories name Hestia as being an Olympian, whereas others include Dionysus instead.

At the head of the Olympians stood Zeus: father of the gods and god of thunder. Despite being the last child of his parents (Rhea and Cronus), Zeus was first among the gods. He is often described as holding a lightning bolt in his right hand, with an eagle perched on his left. He also carries a royal scepter. Zeus is sometimes shown carrying an enormous shield and wearing an oak leaf crown. He has a stately beard and figure and resembles a man well into his adulthood. The Father of the Gods is also seen as the Lord of the Sky and Justice, with control over the weather, fate, and kingship. Zeus was also believed to be the fierce ruler and protector of gods and men. He is the brother of Hera, Demeter, Hades, Hestia, and Poseidon, and the father of the remaining Olympian gods. Zeus gained dominion over the sky after lots were cast among him and his brothers Hades and Poseidon.

Zeus is also married to Hera. However, there are many tales of his unfaithfulness to her. Stories abound of Zeus taking many different forms to couple with humans and other supernatural beings. Those of his children born to mortal women were regarded as demi-gods. These children went on to perform many great acts. In addition to the main gods and demi-gods he sired, Zeus also had The Muses, The Three Graces, Goddesses of the Seasons, and the Fates. His constant unfaithfulness to Hera created constant strife between the two. Zeus would often go to great lengths to hide his amorous activities from her.

Zeus is also said to have had six wives before Hera. Metis (who he later swallowed), Themis, Eurynome, his other sister Demeter, Mnemosyne, and Leto. These women all bore him powerful children.

The people of Ancient Greece both revered and feared Zeus and called on him to protect their homes, families, and property. Zeus was omnipotent and could hurl his lightning bolt from Olympus to strike the guilty anywhere in the world. His pride and callous nature led Hera and several other gods to lead a short-lived rebellion against him. Zeus' punishment of the dissidents was swift and brutal.

Hera

Known as the Queen of the Gods, Hera is associated with marriage, women, and fertility. She is often depicted as modest, matronly, beautiful, and solemn. The cow, cuckoo, and peacock are considered sacred to her. Hera is usually called upon to aid and protect women and children. Her protection especially extends to women in childbirth. Interestingly, it is believed by scholars that her true name is unknown, as 'Hera' is translated to mean 'Lady' or 'Mistress'. Despite being the mother of the gods, Hera is sometimes referred to as a virgin. This is due to the belief that she restores her virginity annually by bathing in a spring.

Her marriage to her youngest brother came about through trickery. It is said that Zeus transformed into an injured cuckoo and presented himself to her. Hera's deep love of animals prompted her into picking up the 'animal' and holding it against her chest to keep it warm. Zeus then resumed his true form and slept with her. Hera, ashamed at being tricked, agreed to marry him. Despite how their marriage began, Hera was deeply faithful to her husband. She was extremely jealous and punished both the women Zeus courted and any children that resulted from his unfaithfulness. Many stories are told of her lying in wait and pursuing him to catch him in the act of cheating. While Zeus felt free to consort with others, he punished anyone who tried to form an intimate relationship with Hera. As a result, despite her great beauty, she remained un-courted by anyone but her husband.

Hera is often depicted as having a strong personality. She is not afraid to stand in opposition to her husband. In fact, she conspired with Poseidon, Athena, and several other gods to drug Zeus and steal his lightning bolt. In punishment, she was hung with golden chains from the sky until she promised never to rebel against Zeus again.

Hera is mainly said to have borne four children with her husband: Ares, Hephaestus, Eileithyia, and Hebe. However, the number changes from anywhere from three to ten depending on the tale.

Demeter

Demeter was believed to be the goddess of agriculture. She was also seen as a goddess of the underworld birth, health, and marriage. Her name indicates she was considered a mother figure. The changing seasons are attributed to her feelings for her daughter with Zeus, Persephone. The story is told of her daughter being kidnapped and taken to the underworld by Hades. Upon hearing the news, Demeter goes searching for her daughter. Her grief was so great that the land grew barren. Zeus eventually intervened as humanity suffered and cried for help while their crops died. Meanwhile, Persephone ate some pomegranate seeds given to her by Hades and doing so required her to spend half the year with Demeter, the other half with Hades in the Underworld. Spring and summer are said to reflect Demeter's joy at having her daughter with her, while fall and winter show her grief as the time her daughter is trapped in the Underworld.

Demeter is commonly depicted as modest, matronly, and regal. She carries a cornucopia and wears a crown of flowers. She is sometimes shown in a chariot with her daughter. Both are shown to carry wheat, ears of corn, scepters, and torches. The festival, Thesmophoria, is an all-female celebration of her. She is also credited with teaching men how to grow and use corn. Two animals sacred to her are the snake and the pig.

Despite being a consort of Zeus, Demeter is said to have had other lovers and have borne children for them.

Poseidon

Poseidon is generally known as the god of the sea. He was also viewed as the god of horses and earthquakes. Poseidon was considered to be violent, temperamental, greedy, vengeful, and hot-blooded. Poseidon is depicted as resembling Zeus and carrying a trident. His shout is as loud as that of ten thousand men. He also rides a chariot pulled by horses. Poseidon is also lustful and did not always require the consent of the women he favored. Like Zeus, he would change forms to seduce or take them forcefully. Despite his many dalliances, he was married to Amphitrite, an Oceanid (a sea nymph).

Poseidon's nature often put him in opposition with both gods and men. He was a part of the rebellion against Zeus and was sent to serve Laomedon, a Trojan king. He also contested Athena over ownership of Athens. They were tasked with providing a gift to the city of Athens, and whoever's gift was considered the best would gain ownership of the city. Poseidon used his trident to strike the ground and create a stream, while Athena created an olive tree. Athena won the contest.

Sailors worshiped him and courted his favor before setting sail. Poseidon is said to be able to create earthquakes by striking his trident on the ground. This aspect of his nature connected him to the land, despite him being a god of the sea. He is said to have a palace of corals and gems, situated on the ocean floor. Poseidon also sired many horses with various women.

Hestia

Hestia is the oldest of the Olympians, and goddess of the hearth. Unlike her more temperamental siblings, she is seen as being pure-hearted and peaceful. Her duty was to stay at Mount

Olympus and tend the fire. Like her sisters, she is portrayed as matronly and modest. She is also often shown wearing a veil and carrying a staff. She is usually depicted as holding flowers or standing near a fire. Her status as goddess of the hearth signified its importance in Greek culture. She is associated with hospitality, happiness, and community, and received the first and best of all offerings. Offerings are made to her at the beginning and end of every meal, and the fire had to be ritually extinguished in her honor.

Hestia was worshiped as a virgin goddess. It is said that both Poseidon and Apollo wanted to marry her. To maintain peace in Olympus, she placed her hand on Zeus' head and swore to remain a virgin forever. Hestia is often substituted with Dionysus in the pantheon.

Aphrodite

Aphrodite is known as the goddess of love, eternal youth, and beauty. There are conflicting stories as to whether she is the aunt or sister of Zeus. As his aunt, her birth was a result of Cronus cutting off his father—Uranus'— genitals and throwing them into the sea. Aphrodite sprang up from the seafoam it landed on. As his daughter, she is said to be the result of his union with the goddess, Dione.

It was said that Aphrodite's beauty was so great that the gods all desired her. To prevent a war, Zeus married her to the "ugly" god, Hephaestus. The union was not Aphrodite's choice, and she had many mortal and immortal lovers, such as Hermes and Dionysus. Her most frequent lover is Ares, god of war. Her most famous child is Eros, better known in Roman mythology as

Cupid, and she often sent him out to shoot both gods and men with his arrows.

Aphrodite is usually depicted naked, with the ideal female face and figure. She is considered to be both desirable and unattainable. She is also known to be vindictive; punishing women who fall in love with Ares, who appear more desirable than she does, and men and women who try to resist her power.

Hephaestus

Hephaestus is known as the god of fire and blacksmiths. He is considered to be ugly. There are two stories about his birth and how he became lame. One claims that he is the son of Zeus and Hera who intervened on his mother's behalf during a quarrel between the couple. In anger, Zeus cast him from the heavens, breaking his legs. The other story states that Hera conceived and birthed Hephaestus herself to get back at Zeus for having Athena. Horrified of his deformed looks, she then cast him out into the world, breaking his legs. He was rescued and sheltered by sea nymphs until he reclaimed his place in Olympus.

Despite his appearance, Hephaestus is known for crafting beautiful things. His forge was a volcano, and he made many of the weapons the gods wielded. Hephaestus also created their homes and furniture and had assistants made of gold. He is typically depicted as being either young or in his middle years, with unkempt hair. He is also married to Aphrodite.

Athena

Athena is known as the goddess of wisdom, weaving, and war. Her birth was a bit unusual, even for the gods. Zeus's first wife, Metis, was prophesied to deliver a son who would grow more powerful than he was. To avoid that, Zeus swallowed his wife. However, Metis was already pregnant with Athena. One day, Zeus complained of a terrible headache. His son, Hephaestus, hit his head with a hammer and an adult Athena sprang out, clothed in armor. Her cry was ferocious, and Zeus was filled with pride. She was known as his favorite both for her fierce nature, and because he birthed her himself.

Athena is often shown in armor or wearing an ancient dress and carrying a shield with Medusa's head at its center. She is shown to be stern, beautiful, and authoritative, with gray eyes. She is also depicted carrying a spear and wearing a Corinthian-style helmet. An owl often sits on her shoulder, denoting her role as the goddess of wisdom. She is also shown with a spindle in her hand, representing her role as the goddess of handicraft.

Despite being the goddess of warfare, Athena did not have a blood-thirsty nature. Instead, she believed in solving problems through intelligence and diplomacy, with war being a last resort. And even then, she believed that war should only be fought for noble and just causes. She is shown as being more powerful than her brother, Ares, who was also a god of war. Athena is also known as the virgin goddess as she never married or took a lover.

Ares

Ares is known as the god of war. He is destructive and cruel, and it is said that he is unloved by all except Aphrodite. His own parents, Zeus and Hera, detested him. Unlike Athena, Ares is said to partake in unnecessary, bloody wars. He is often depicted wearing a helmet and carrying weapons. He rides in a chariot drawn by four horses, and he is accompanied by vultures. Ares is said to be cowardly, displaying outrage at any injury he receives. He is the father of the Amazons and Aphrodite's main lover. Ares is usually shown to be humiliated in stories.

Artemis

Artemis is known as the goddess of the moon, the hunt, chastity, and nature. Artemis is also known for curing the diseases of women, protecting children, and aiding in childbirth. She is the daughter of Zeus and Leto, and the older twin sister of Apollo. Artemis is fiercely protective of her twin. It is said that a jealous Hera cursed their mother so that she would never give birth on land. Leto gave birth on a floating island and when Artemis was born, she aided in the birth of her brother.

Artemis is one of the most loved and respected gods. She is depicted as a young huntress, carrying a bow and with a hunting dog at her side. In her role as goddess of the moon, she wears a crescent moon crown and a long robe. When she was still young, she asked Zeus that she be allowed to keep her virginity forever. She became fiercely protective of her maidenhood, and those of her priestesses. The gods were also protective of her virginity and attacked anyone who dared touch her when she was unable to defend herself.

Apollo

Apollo is known as the god of the sun, prophecy, healing, the arts, knowledge, beauty, order, plagues, agriculture, and archery. He is the younger twin of Artemis. Apollo is considered the perfect specimen of masculinity. He is often depicted as youthful and athletic, wearing a laurel crown, and carrying a bow and arrow or a lyre. Apollo became the god of music after his brother, Hermes, stole his cattle. In apology, Hermes gave him the lyre, which he (Hermes) had invented.

Apollo is credited with teaching men the art of healing. He was also granted the gift of prophecy due to his faithfulness, honesty, and integrity. He had many male and female lovers, though his affairs usually ended in tragedy.

Hermes

Hermes was known as the messenger god, and the god of thieves, flocks, travelers, athletes, and trade. He is the son of Zeus and the nymph, Maia. It was said that a few days after his birth, Hermes invented the lyre. He then went out and stole his brother Apollo's cows and covered their tracks. However, Apollo hunted him down and he traded his lyre for the cows. He is known to be both fast and clever and is considered a trickster god. He is also the only one of the twelve Olympians who can freely travel between the land of the living and the dead. Hermes is also seen as a guide in the underworld. It is said that Hermes invented speech. The gods loved him and several of them taught him how to hunt and play the pipes. He often accompanied Zeus on his trysts, delivered messages to his lovers, and covered for him with Hera.

Hermes is depicted as an athletic youth with winged sandals. He wears a broad-brimmed hat and carries a caduceus (two snakes winding around a short, winged staff). Hermes appears in many tales as a messenger of the gods and a guide to heroes.

Dionysus

Dionysus is sometimes called the 'party god'. He is the god of wine and fertility. Dionysus often replaces Hestia in the Greek pantheon. He is the son of Zeus and Semele, a mortal woman. Zeus appeared to Semele as an invisible entity, and she welcomed his affections. However, Hera tricked her into wanting to see Zeus' form. A pregnant Semele convinced Zeus under oath to reveal himself, but when he did, his glory turned her to ash. Zeus took the fetus and sewed it into his thigh until Dionysus matured enough to be born. Dionysus was later killed by Titans who ripped him apart on Hera's orders. However, his grandmother, Rhea, resurrected him, and Zeus hid him among the mountain nymphs.

Dionysus wandered the earth, teaching men about wine. He was accompanied by wild women called the Maenads. His followers often entered a state of religious ecstasy and madness. Dionysus was worshiped alongside Demeter as one of the major gods of the earth. He is depicted as a semi-naked (or naked) youth with feminine features. Dionysus was the last god to join the Greek pantheon. He married the mortal princess, Ariadne.

Hades

Hades is known as the god of the Underworld. He is also referred to as the god of wealth as gems and precious metals were dug up from the ground. Hades is not considered to be one of the Olympians, but he is still seen as the brother of Zeus and the others. The Ancient Greeks viewed Hades with reverence and terror. He is said to rarely leave the Underworld. and is usually referred to as being at one with his realm. He is shown as a bearded, mournful figure wearing a helmet and carrying a two-pronged weapon called a bident. Occasionally, he carries the keys to his kingdom or a staff and rides a chariot. Cerberus (the three-headed dog who guards the door to the Underworld) is typically by his side. In representation of his status as the god of wealth, he is also usually shown carrying a cornucopia.

Hades' role in judgment and punishment was supervisory. The actual torture was carried out by creatures called the furies. Like Hestia, his nature differs from that of his siblings. He is aloof and cannot be swayed by sacrifice. His personality was as unmoving as death. Hades was sometimes called 'the other Zeus' by Ancient Greeks. They believed that eventually, all men ended up serving him in his realm. Hades rarely interfered with the land of the living and jealously guarded his dead. While he defended their rights, he was easily angered should any of his souls seek to escape or be rescued by others.

The Greeks feared him and often referred to him by his kingdom. He was depicted in very little art and stories. The most famous story of him is the one where he fell in love with and kidnapped his wife, Persephone.

Chapter 2: Men and Monsters

Greek mythology is rife with stories of heroes, sinners, witches, and monsters. All these entities are heavily influenced by the gods. The children of the gods went on to perform great deeds and great cruelty. For their efforts, they were either rewarded or damned.

Heracles

Heracles is considered to be the mightiest Greek hero. He has long been upheld as an example of strength, bravery, and masculinity. According to Greek mythology, his deeds, dedication, and triumphs despite opposition earned him a place among the gods. Despite the positive views of this aspect of his personality, Heracles is depicted as being short-tempered and impulsive. His superhuman strength is credited to Zeus being his father. The blood of the hero Perseus also ran through his veins by way of his mother, Alcmene (Perseus' granddaughter). Being the son of Zeus also led to him being a target of Hera. The jealous goddess tried many times to destroy him even before he was born. The greatest story of Heracles is the tale of the twelve labors he was ordered to complete as punishment for killing his first wife and children. We'll get to that story later!

Perseus

Perseus is considered to be one of the oldest heroes in Greek mythology. He is said to have been the son of Princess Danae and Zeus. It is said that while Danae was asleep, Zeus appeared to her in a shower of gold and slept with her. The young demi-god grew up in relative peace until a king sought to get rid of him so he—the king—could have Perseus' mother. Perseus is credited with killing Medusa with the guidance of Athena and Hermes. It is also said that he created the Atlas mountains by turning the giant, Atlas, into stone.

Aeacus

Aeacus is considered to be one of the three judges of the underworld. However, this role was taken up after his death. In his mortal life, he was the king of Aegina. Aeacus is said to be the son of Zeus and a river god's daughter by the name of Aegina. Zeus brought Aegina to an uninhabited land—which later was named in her honor—where she gave birth to Aeacus. One version of the story claims the island was naturally without men, while the other blames Hera for driving off the men with a plague. Whatever the cause, Zeus turned all the ants into men, giving rise to the race, the Myrmidons.

Aeacus was praised by his people as being a fair and just king. Both gods and men from all across Greece sought his counsel. His judgment was highly respected. As a result of this, he carried on passing judgment in the Underworld when he died.

Achilles

The warrior, Achilles was the son of the mortal, Peleus—a Myrmidon king—and the water nymph, Thetis. Thetis, in an attempt to make Achilles invincible, dipped him in the River Styx. However, she held him by his heel to do so. As a result, his entire body was invincible other than his heel, which became his only weak point. This story eventually led to the body part being called the 'Achilles tendon', a term that is still used today. Achilles was raised hidden from the world and disguised as a girl during his formative years. However, he eventually joined the Trojan war, fighting on the side of the Grecian king, Agamemnon.

During much of the ten years of the war, Achilles was a critical factor. He sacked many cities and killed the Trojan prince, Troilus. This was significant for the Greeks as it had been prophesied that the city of Troy would fall if the prince died before his 20th birthday. However, Achilles departed from the war for a time as King Agamemnon insulted him by taking his newly captured lover. The Greeks suffered in battle due to this, and both the king and his friend begged him to rejoin the war. Achilles refused until he received word that his friend had been killed in battle. A grieving and enraged Achilles re-entered the fray. However, Apollo interfered, sending Prince Paris' (the one who was responsible for the beginnings of the war) arrow directly into Achilles' heel. The blow killed the mighty warrior.

Hector

Hector was the crown prince of Troy and their greatest warrior. He was against the Trojan war and tried to broker peace with the Greeks. However, his efforts were in vain. He was said to be a good man, son, father, husband, and prince. He was also said to have been loved by Apollo. Hector was known for fighting valiantly and showing respect to his opponents. Unfortunately, he enraged Achilles after he killed Achilles' friend, Patroclus. They dueled, and Hector grew afraid and ran. However, he eventually decided to turn and face his fate. Achilles killed him and dragged his body behind his chariot for twelve days. The Trojans ultimately reclaimed him and buried him with honor.

Theseus

One of Athens' earliest kings, Theseus was a mighty hero. He was considered a brave and just defender, the epitome of a man of Athens. While it is clear that his mother was the princess Aethra, there is some dispute about who his true father was. While he was accepted as being King Aegeus of Athens' son, it was also said by some that he was the son of Poseidon. Theseus is most famed for defeating the minotaur of the labyrinth.

Jason

Unlike many of the heroes in Greek mythology, Jason was not a demi-god. He was the son of King Aeson and Queen Alcimede. However, his half-uncle Pelias stole the throne. To keep him safe, Jason was sent to live in isolation. Unlike heroes who were the illegitimate children of Zeus, Jason gained the aid of Hera. She guided him during his quest to recover the golden fleece. The quest had been given to him by his uncle, who feared Jason because of a prophecy telling him to beware of someone matching Jason's description. Jason's journey was aided by a group of brave men and women called the Argonauts. One of these Argonauts was the hero, Heracles. They set out by ship and overcame many obstacles to attain their prize.

Odysseus

Odysseus is the hero of Homer's famous epic tale, the Odyssey. Like Jason, he was born to mortal parents, Laertes and Anticlea. Odysseus was brave, resourceful, cunning, charismatic, and wise. He was known as an eloquent speaker, masterful strategist, and trickster. However, his cleverness proved to be his undoing. Odysseus presented himself as one of the many suitors of Helen of Troy. After giving up hope of winning her, he provided a solution to her stepfather on how to maintain peace among her suitors. He told the king—Helen's stepfather— to have each suitor swear an oath to protect whoever was chosen to be Helen's husband.

When Helen was stolen, Odysseus was called upon to fight as one of her former suitors. However, Odysseus was happy with his wife, Penelope. He was also aware of a prophecy that stated he would go through many trials and be gone for many years. He tried to escape the conscription by feigning madness but was found out. Eventually, he agreed to join the war. Odysseus proved to be a formidable military tactician and performed well during the battle.

Unfortunately, the journey home took ten years. During that time, he angered Poseidon, encountered a witch, and had many dangerous adventures. When he returned home, twenty years after he had left, he found his wife beset by suitors. Odysseus killed them all and reclaimed his throne.

Orpheus

Orpheus was the son of King Oegrus of Thrace and the muse, Calliope. His mother's blood made him a skilled and famous poet, musician, and prophet. He mastered the lyre under the tutelage of Apollo. He was so skilled that nature danced to his music. Orpheus was one of the Argonauts and it was his music that saved them from the Sirens. He later met and married Eurydice. Unfortunately, she stepped into a viper's nest and died after being bitten. Orpheus was unable to accept her death and traveled to the underworld, playing his music all the way. He charmed Charon and put Cerberus to sleep. Persephone was delighted by his devotion and music and convinced Hades to give him a chance to rescue his wife. Hades agreed on the condition that Orpheus lead Eurydice out of the underworld without once looking back. Unfortunately, Orpheus gave in to temptation and Eurydice was whisked back to the underworld. Orpheus was forced to live without her, but they were eventually reunited upon his death.

Chiron

Chiron was the son of a titan, the first centaur, and Zeus' half-brother. His father, Cronus, was unfaithful to his wife Rhea, and slept with the nymph Philyra. To escape Rhea's wrath, Cronus transformed into a horse. Chiron was born half-man, half-horse as a result of this. Unlike the other centaurs, his forelegs were human. He was also kind, learned, and civilized whereas other centaurs were violent and prone to indulgence. Chiron was famed for his wisdom and teaching ability. He tutored heroes such as Heracles, Achilles, and Jason. His immortality was lost when he was accidentally shot with a poisoned arrow by Heracles. Bleeding and in pain, he gave up his immortality to free Prometheus at the request of the very student who shot him.

Charon

Charon was known as the ferryman of the dead and the son of Nyx and Erebus. It was said that when Hermes gathered up the souls of the dead, he would escort them to the Rivers Acheron and Styx. Charon would then ferry them across to the underworld. He charged each soul one coin to carry them across. Ancient Greeks made sure to leave this coin with their dead as it was believed he would refuse to carry any who could not pay his fee. These people wandered the world as ghosts. Charon is described as being very ugly, with a crooked nose and a beard. He wears a conical hat and is often depicted steering his boat.

Prometheus

Prometheus is the son of the Titan Iapetus and Clymene the nymph. He was known as the god of fire and the first and ultimate trickster. He was highly intelligent, and a craftsman. In the fight between the Olympians, Prometheus joined the younger gods and devised the plan that led to the Titan's defeat. However, he later defied the gods and gifted man with the knowledge of fire. As punishment, Zeus chained him and had an eagle feast on his constantly regenerated liver. He was eventually freed by Heracles and made peace with Zeus.

Atlas

Atlas was the brother of Prometheus and the son of Iapetus and Clymene. He was the leader of the Titan rebellion and was punished by Zeus to forever hold up the sky. Atlas was briefly freed from this duty by Heracles, who tricked him into once again bearing up the sky on his shoulders. Eventually, the hero Perseus used Medusa's head to turn Atlas into stone. He became known as Mount Atlas.

Typhon

The son of Tartarus and Gaia was a fearsome being and the father of all monsters. He is described as being tall enough to touch the stars, and his torso was human. Typhon had a hundred viper's legs and arms, and dragon heads. His eyes glowed red and he had hundreds of wings. His human head had pointed ears and a matted beard. Typhon had black skin and was completely filthy. It was said that some of his heads were of different animals like bulls and boars. The coils of his hands stretched from east to west and fire churned from his mouth. His birth is sometimes credited to Hera, who is said to have wanted to create a being more powerful than Zeus. However, Typhon was defeated by Zeus and thrown into the Underworld.

He was married to Echidna, and together they had several children including the Sphinx, Cerberus, Hydra, and Chimera. Typhon is associated with volcanic forces and dangerous winds.

Echidna

The wife of Typhon was described as having the upper body of a woman while her lower half was that of a serpent. The tales of Echidna's origins are a bit unclear. Some state that she was a child of Gaia and Tartarus, while others say her parents were Ceto and Phorcys. Echidna was associated with corruption (rot, disease, foul waters, slime) of the earth. She was born and raised in a cave and ate passing travelers. Both Echidna and her husband, Typhon, were held in terror and awe by the ancient Greeks.

The Sirens

The Sirens are the daughters of a Muse and Achelous the river god. They were described as being a combination of women and birds. While their faces were human, their bodies were that of birds. Their transformation from full nymphs to part bird was credited to Demeter. One tale states that they aided Demeter in her quest to find Persephone and were granted wings to fly as a reward. Other stories suggest that they transformed into birds as a punishment.

The sisters lived on three rocky, small islands with the rotting corpses of their victims strewn about. They sang passing sailors to their deaths. Their singing was enchanting, but no match for the Muses who won a singing challenge against them and then plucked out their feathers and turned them into crowns. It was prophesied that they would die if a mortal survived their song. The Argonauts escaped them when the hero, Orpheus, drowned out their singing by playing his music. The sirens survived this encounter but were defeated by Odysseus who had his sailors plug their ears with wax and tie him to the mast of his ship as he sailed past their home. The sirens threw themselves to their deaths.

Chapter 3: The Creation of Gods and Men

Like all religions, the Greeks had their own stories of how the world began. To them, the universe they knew came about as a result of birth, chaos, and war.

In the Beginning

The world began with the vast nothingness of Chaos. From Chaos rose the first two primordial gods, Erebus and Nyx. Both were beings of darkness and silence, yet from them sprung Eros (love), Aether (the upper air), and Hemera (day). However, everyone feared Nyx and shunned her. Unloved by all but her brother, she birthed children on her own, so she would have a family to love her. The names of some of these children were Thanatos (death), Ker (doom), Geras (old age), Hypnos (sleep), Oneiroi (dreams), Oizus (pain), and several others.

Chaos gave birth again and Gaia, the earth; and Tartarus, the underworld, came into being. By herself, Gaia gave birth to Uranus (the heavens). The earth and the heavens became mates and birthed the twelve Titans, three Cyclops, and the three Hecatoncheires (hundred-handed ones). But Uranus did not love his children. Instead, he imprisoned them deep within Gaia's womb. In anger, Gaia tried to incite her children against her husband. All except the youngest, Cronus, were too afraid. Taking up the great sickle his mother had fashioned, he cut off his father's genitals as he was about to sleep with his mother. The blood from the castration fell on the earth and produced the Furies, the Ash Tree Nymphs (the Meliae), and the giants. When his genitals fell into the sea it is said that Aphrodite, the goddess of love, came into being. This act separated heaven and the earth and Uranus vanished. As he left, he promised a great reckoning would befall the Titans for what Cronus had done.

As the new ruler of the universe, Cronus imprisoned the Hecantoncheires and the Cyclops. He then married his sister, Rhea. Under their rule, the Titans flourished and reproduced. From them came the nymphs, river gods, the sun, moon, dawn, and many more. But Uranus' words could not be denied. A prophecy was made that Cronus would be killed by one of his sons. To avoid this, Cronus swallowed each of his children as they were born. Hades, Hestia, Demeter, Hera, and Poseidon were all wrested from their mother and devoured. Like Gaia, Rhea was enraged at what had been done to her children and sought revenge. She hid herself when it was time for her to give birth to her sixth child, Zeus, and left him in the care of the nymphs. She then swaddled a stone and gave it to Cronus to swallow. The god did so and left, thinking he had averted disaster.

Raised by a nymph and a goat, Zeus grew into a strong young man and sought out Metis (wisdom). With her guidance, he devised a plan to defeat his father. Metis prepared a wine that would cause the god to vomit, and Zeus disguised himself as his father's cupbearer. After gaining Cronus' trust, Zeus slipped him what Cronus thought was his favorite wine. Cronus vomited out Omphalos, known as the Navel, and his five children. In gratitude, these children recognized Zeus as their leader despite him being the youngest.

But the threat of their father remained. He had grown weak with age but sought out the help of his siblings, the Titans. These Titans feared the new gods and rallied against them at Cronus' command. A bitter battle was fought for over a decade, with the

Titans winning many victories. This ten-year war became known as the Titanomachy. The Titans were led by Atlas and fought from their home on Mount Othrys. However, not all of them agreed with the older god's desire to rule. Two Titans, Prometheus, and Themis sided with the younger gods. With the guidance of Gaia, they helped turn the tide in the Olympians' favor.

Gaia guided Zeus into traveling to the underworld and freeing the Hecantoncheires and the Cyclops. This finally set her children free, and they joined the battle. Prometheus designed the plan that led to victory. The Olympians engaged the Titans while the Hecantoncheires laid an ambush. Zeus drew the Titans into their trap with a strategic retreat. The Hecantoncheires rained down boulders upon the Titan's heads until they ran away. Zeus claimed the throne of the universe and exiled the Titans, locking them away in Tartarus. Atlas, however, was forced to bear up the sky on his shoulders for eternity. This ended the Titanomachy, but this was not really the end. Once again outraged at the imprisonment of her children, Gaia gave birth to the terrifying Typhon. Using his thunderbolts, Zeus defeated him in battle and sealed him under the earth. It is said that he growls beneath the volcano of Mount Etna, waiting for the moment he will rise again to face Zeus.

The Ages of Men

As the gods rose and fell, so did the ones they created. The Greeks believed there were five great ages of men and their evolution. While Cronus reigned, he created man and made him perfect. The people lived in eternal spring and aged backward. Dying was like falling asleep, and then they roamed the earth as ghosts. Men lived like gods and knew no sorrow, pain, and toil. The gods provided for their every need, and all was peaceful. It was a time of beauty and perfection that ended with the rise of the Olympians.

The world then entered the Silver era, where Zeus diminished the appearance and wisdom of man and created the four seasons of the year. Man no longer walked in concert with the gods and was forced to labor and create shelters. Despite this, children kept their innocence and were free to frolic for the first hundred years of their lives. However, man no longer honored the gods as they used to, and Zeus grew furious. He made death a part of their lives and decreed they would descend to the Underworld as blessed spirits upon their passing.

This toil and turmoil increased with the Bronze Age. Zeus used ash trees to form man. These men were terrible and hard. They ate mainly meat and went to war with each other. Their houses and weapons were made of bronze, and fighting consumed their entire existence. They were soulless and languished in the Underworld after death. Finally, a great flood arose and washed the earth clean of them.

And then came the Age of Heroes. Pandora had had a daughter named Pyrrha, who had married Prometheus' son, Deucalion. They were the only survivors of the flood and created men out of stones to repopulate the earth. During this time, demigods abounded, and man did great deeds. It was in the Age of Heroes that man came closest to what they were before. Heroes like Achilles, Heracles, and many others inspired their fellow men and led their people to victory over their enemies with the favor and aid of the Olympians. However, many of these heroes died in wars or as a result of their actions and hubris. Men and women who were brave and honored the gods entered the paradise,

Elysium, when they died. The unjust and blasphemers were punished in the Underworld.

Finally, there was the Iron Age. The distance between god and man caused man to suffer. They became more selfish, greedy, and duplicitous. Brother turned against brother and all pretense of observing the law disappeared. The virtues and the gods themselves were abandoned. In response, the gods left the earth to their suffering. And so, man lives on in toil and misery until Zeus will finally destroy the human race and start anew.

Prometheus and Pandora

When the Golden Age ended, man grew very discontented with the gods. They murmured against them and taught their children to do the same. In anger, Zeus kept the knowledge of fire from them. Mankind could not survive without this knowledge, and so their very existence was threatened. The Titan Prometheus saw their suffering and sympathized with them. He stole one of Zeus' lightning bolts and used it to teach man about fire. Zeus was enraged and chained Prometheus to a rock. Prometheus' punishments were many. Storms lashed at him, and the sun burnt his flesh. An eagle appeared daily to eat his liver, which would regenerate each day. Prometheus suffered this fate for a thousand years.

But Zeus' anger was not appeased. He determined that man must also be punished for what had been done. And so, the first woman was created. She was fashioned from clay by Hephaestus and given femininity by Aphrodite. Athena taught her handicrafts while Hermes taught her curiosity and deceit. The gods named her Pandora and saw her as human perfection.

They also gave her a jar -later called a box- of "special gifts". However, they warned her never to open it. She was then given to Epimetheus, who was Prometheus' brother. Despite his brother's warning never to accept gifts from the gods, Epimetheus fell in love with Pandora's beauty and married her. At first, Pandora tried to be strong and keep the box closed as the gods had advised her. However, her curiosity won out and she opened the box. The results were devastating. Death, sickness, envy, strife, and many others escaped to fill the land and bring pain and anguish to man. When Pandora saw the evils escaping, she snapped the box shut. However, it was too late. Everything had escaped, and only hope remained trapped inside. This was by Zeus' design, as he wanted man to suffer for their disrespect of the gods.

Chapter 4: Perseus

Acrisius, King of Argos, was told by the Oracle of Delphi that he would be killed by his grandson. Now, Acrisius had cheated his twin brother out of his inheritance. His ambition was great, and he had no intention of forfeiting his life or his kingdom, so, he locked his daughter, Danae, away in a bronze chamber underground, far from any man who would seduce her. The chamber had no windows, and the King thought he was safe from the prophecy. However, her beauty caught Zeus' eye. Turning into a shower of gold, he slipped into her chamber through a crack in the roof and slept with her. Danae became pregnant but was able to keep it from her father as he rarely visited. When he finally arrived, she had already given birth. Acrisius was enraged. He refused to believe she had been visited by the Father of the Gods. When Danae gave birth, the King locked her and her baby boy into a wooden chest and had them thrown into the sea.

But the gods took note and guided them through turbulent waters to the island of Seriphos. The King of the island's brother, Dictys, happened to be fishing, and the chest got caught in his net. The humble fisherman and prince brought the two into his home and raised Perseus as his own. Dictys knew how the two would be viewed by the Seripheans and their king, so he hid them away from prying eyes. Several years passed before anyone learned of their existence. His brother, King Polydectes, fell madly in love with Danae. He wooed her with words and gifts, but the shy, sheltered princess refused his suit. The proud king refused to take no for an answer. He saw her son, Perseus as an obstacle to getting what he wanted and so he resolved to be rid of him. If Perseus was gone, he reasoned, there would be no one to stop him from taking Danae.

So Polydectes devised a plan. He feigned an engagement with Hippodamia, Princess of Pisa. In honor of this engagement, everyone living in Seriphos was required to gift him a horse. However, Perseus was from a foreign land. He had no horses or money to buy one. His pride prompted him to offer something else.

"Ask anything of me, King Polydectes," he said. "And I will bring it to you."

This made King Polydectes smile. Perseus' offer was exactly what he had intended.

"Instead of a horse, bring me Medusa's head," he declared.

Now, Medusa was a Gorgon, the granddaughter of Gaia. Unlike her other, monstrous sisters, she was a beautiful mortal. Poseidon was so struck by her loveliness that he slept with her at Athena's temple. The goddess was outraged by this and transformed Medusa into a hideous being. Her once lovely hair became snakes and her gaze turned men to stone. She grew tusks and fangs and became the ugliest of her sisters. Polydetes believed that sending Perseus after her would be condemning the young man to his death. However, he would be free of blame. After all, Perseus had offered to bring the King anything he desired.

Perseus knew how dangerous this quest was, but he could not refuse. He had given his word. And so, he set off in search of Medusa. He wandered the land to no avail, and eventually gave in to despair. Seeing his plight, two gods took pity on him and appeared to him. The female was tall, grey-eyed, and solemn, while the male was mischievous and wore winged sandals.

"I am Athena, and this is Hermes," explained the woman. "We have come to aid you in your quest."

"To find Medusa, you need to seek out her sisters, the Graeae; they will tell you where to go," said Hermes.

Hermes then gifted him with a sword, while Athena gave him her shield. So armed, Perseus set out to do as they had advised. He found the cave of the Graeae and peered in. The sisters had stringy grey hair and shared a single tooth and eye amongst themselves. Perseus laid in wait until one of them took out the eye to pass it to another. He immediately rose up and snatched the eye.

"I will not return it until you tell me where I can Medusa," he told them.

They agreed. "Go to the Stygian Nymphs, they will lead you to her." In addition to directions, they gave him Hades' invisibility cap, winged sandals, and a magical bag to hold Medusa's dead – though some versions of the tale suggest these items were instead given to Perseus by Athena and Hermes. Regardless, Perseus now knew where to go and was well armed. He returned their eye and went on his way.

The nymphs revealed Medusa's location to him. He found her and her sisters sleeping in a cave. Perseus used his shield as a reflection to prevent himself from looking the mortal-turned monster in the eye. The winged sandals made his progress swift and silent while the cap made him invisible. Athena, still angry with Medusa, guided his hand. With one stroke, Perseus cut off Medusa's head and placed it in the bag. However, the Gorgon had been impregnated by Poseidon. Her children came forth from her neck; the golden warrior Chrysaor, and the winged horse Pegasus. The noise of their birth woke the other two Gorgons. Seeing their sister dead, they wailed and tried to attack Perseus. However, he was invisible, and they were unable to harm him. Their cries were so loud and mournful that even the vengeful Athena was moved. She created the double pipe -the aulos- to mimic their weeping.

Having completed his quest, Perseus began his journey home. After a long time, he came to where Atlas was holding the sky up on his shoulders. Exhausted and thirsty, he asked the Titan for food and shelter for the night. But Atlas had been told that someone would one day come to trick him and steal his apples. In fear of this prophecy, he refused to aid Perseus. In anger, Perseus took out Medusa's head. One look turned the giant into stone. Perseus put the head back in the bag and continued on.

His path took him through Ethiopia where he saw a sight that shocked him. A beautiful young woman was chained to a rock by the sea. Perseus fell deeply in love with her. He discovered that she was Princess Andromeda, and went to her father, King Cephus, to ask for her hand in marriage. But the princess was a virgin sacrifice meant to save the people. Her mother, Queen Cassiopeia, had declared that she was more beautiful than the sea nymphs, called Nereids. These nymphs were the wards of Poseidon and they complained to him in bitter anger. Poseidon heard their complaints and sent the sea monster, Cetus, to plague Ethiopia's coast. In desperation, King Cephus appealed to Zeus for aid. The god told him that the only way to free themselves was to chain the innocent Andromeda to a rock. This they had done, and now they were waiting for the monster to take her.

After hearing the story, Perseus made a deal with the king. He would rescue the princess and in turn, the king would give his approval for them to marry. King Cephus agreed. Perseus returned to the sea and waited for Cetus to appear. The monster rose from the sea, drooling in anticipation of his meal. As he had with Medusa, Perseus sliced his head off and freed the princess.

King Cephus honored his agreement and was pleased to be gaining a courageous son-in-law.

However, his brother Phineus was not happy. He had initially been promised Andromeda's hand and felt he deserved to have her now that she would no longer be sacrificed. Gathering his allies, he challenged the king. This angered Perseus who was not only in love with Andromeda but did not believe that anyone who turned away and allowed her to be sacrificed had a right to her. He told King Cephus and his allies to look away and then took out Medusa's head. Everyone who listened to his warning was spared, but Phineus and his comrades were turned to stone. Perseus and Andromeda were now free to wed. They did so happily, and Perseus continued home with his new wife.

Finally, he arrived at the island of Seriphos. There he learned from his adopted father Dictys that his mother was being pursued by Polydectes despite her many refusals. This harassment of his mother made him furious. He stormed the palace and interrupted the feast King Polydectes was having with his attendants. Once again, he took out Medusa's head and everyone in the dining hall turned to stone. They were frozen in the act of eating and Danae was finally free. Perseus then put Dictys on the throne as king of Seriphos.

By this time Perseus had learned of his heritage. He, his wife, and his mother traveled to Argos to make peace with King Acrisius. His grandfather heard of his coming and recalled the prophecy that one of his grandsons would kill him. Fearing his life, the king fled. Perseus and his family soon learned of Acrisius' departure and continued on their way. Along his journey, the young hero heard of a sports competition and traveled there to compete. His discus throw was so powerful it flew into the audience and struck an old man, killing him. Perseus learned that the man he had just killed was his own grandfather.

The throne of Argos was passed on to Perseus after his grandfather's death. Perseus refused in shame and guilt and buried the old king. He went to his cousin, King Megapenthes, and offered a trade: he would rule Tiryns - which was Megapenthes' kingdom - and Megapenthes would rule Argos. The king agreed to the deal and the two switched kingdoms. Perseus went on to live happily with Andromeda. They had many children, and he eventually founded the kingdom of Mycenae.

Chapter 5: The Life and Labors of Heracles

The Early Life of Greece's Greatest Hero

The mighty hero Heracles was yet another product of Zeus' wondering eye. The god desired Queen Alcmene, the granddaughter of Perseus, and slept with her while disguised as her husband, Amphitryon. However, her husband also slept with her that night and she became pregnant with twins. Hera heard of this infidelity and was enraged. She devised a plan to punish Zeus and destroy the child.

When the twins were born, she was unable to identify which one was her husband's bastard son. She sent two snakes into the crib where the babies lay together. Both babies reacted differently. Iphicles, Heracles' twin, cried while Heracles strangled both snakes without hesitation, proving he was Zeus' child. From then on, Hera focused her jealous rage on him.

His mother, Alcmene, feared Hera's wrath and made the difficult decision to abandon her son in a field. But Zeus sent Athena to intervene. The goddess of wisdom brought the baby to Hera and told her she had rescued a strange child. Despite her vengeful nature, Hera was still a mother. She took Heracles and nursed him on her breast. But baby Heracles was strong and eager, and he bit down too hard on her nipple. The pain caused Hera to pull him away and her milk sprayed out, creating the Milky Way. Athena took the child and presented him to Alcmene and Amphitryon. The king and queen realized the gods would protect Heracles and so they gladly kept him.

Heracles grew to be a strong, proud, and passionate young man. Those around him taught him archery, boxing, wrestling, how to drive chariots, writing, music, and fencing. The centaur Chiron taught him wisdom. Heracles wanted for nothing as a child and excelled in all that he did. His first heroic act came when the Thespian lion preyed on Amphitryon's herds and those of his neighbor, King Thespius. Heracles pulled an olive tree up from the ground and turned it into a club. Club in hand, he hunted the lion for fifty days and slew it.

King Thespius was in awe of the strength and bravery of the young prince who had just attained manhood. He decided that his kingdom would be strong if all of his daughters bore Heracles' children. Thespius welcomed Heracles into his home with honor. For fifty nights that Heracles searched for the lion, King Thespius sent each of his daughters to sleep with the young hero. Heracles was unable to tell the difference between the fifty sisters. He believed he slept each night with the same one. All fifty princesses conceived and bore his children.

After his adventures with the lion and the princesses, Heracles continued his journey home. On his way, he encountered the Herolds of King Erginus. Now Erginus was furious with the Thebans due to his father's murder. He went to war with Thebes and slew many of its people. He then forced them into a treaty that required them to pay him a hundred oxen every year for twenty years. It was during the yearly collection of this tribute that Heracles crossed paths with the Herolds. Once he had learned of their purpose, he cut off their hands, ears, and noses. These he then tied them around their necks and sent them back to their king.

"This is the tribute," he told them, "Carry this back to King Erginus."

This further angered the King who gathered his army and marched against Thebes. Heracles met him in battle and defeated him. Heracles' defense of Thebes caused a grateful King Creon to give his daughter, Megara, to Heracles as his wife. The two married and had several children together.

But Hera had been watching and biding her time. Seeing Heracles happy and hailed as a hero, she resolved once again to destroy him. This time she struck him with madness. Heracles lost himself and killed his wife and children. When he regained his senses, he was devastated. He decided to kill himself out of guilt and despair but Theseus, his cousin, convinced him otherwise.

"Suicide is the coward's way out," Theseus told him. "Far better to live and atone for your sins."

So, Heracles went to the Oracle of Delphi to find out what he should do to show his repentance for his crimes and to make restitution. The Oracle sent him to his cousin, King Eurystheus.

The Twelve Labors of Heracles

As his punishment, the Oracle said that Heracles was to be Eurystheus' servant for twelve years. If during that time he completed ten labors, then he would be granted immortality. Heracles considered his cousin to be beneath him and was unhappy with what he had been told to do but complied with what the Oracle said. King Eurystheus was also at odds with his cousin. The king plotted with Hera to kill Heracles. It was with glee that he gave Heracles his first task.

King Eurystheus declared that Heracles should rid Nemea of a monstrous lion. The child of Typhon and Echidna, the Nemean lion terrorized Nemea. The lion took many women hostage, prompting courageous men to attempt to rescue these women. However, anyone who entered the lion's cave to free the hostages was killed and eaten.

Heracles met a young boy on his way to complete his first labor. The boy asked him to kill the lion.

"A lion will be sacrificed to Zeus if the beast is killed within one month," the boy said, "otherwise, I will sacrifice myself."

Heracles accepted the boy's request and proceeded to hunt the lion. When he found it, he shot it full of arrows. Unfortunately, the hide could not be pierced by any sharp object. Heracles then decided to follow the lion to its home. There, he blocked one entrance and snuck in through the other. He had to feel around in the dark to find the lion and once he did, he stunned it with his club. Heracles then used his bare hands to strangle the lion to death. The invincible skin of the lion impressed him so much that he decided to use it as armor. However, he had no way of removing it until Athena guided him in using the lion's claws to skin the beast. Heracles clothed himself in the lion's pelt, used its scalp as a helmet, and returned home.

Despite being the High King of two countries and the grandson of the great hero, Perseus, Eurystheus was weak and cowardly. He fled upon his cousin's approach, thinking that the lion had come to take revenge on him. However, he soon realized that it was Heracles wearing the lion's hide and sent him on his second task.

This time, Heracles was asked to slay the Lernaean Hydra. Hera had raised the monster in a poisonous swamp so that it would one day kill Heracles. The beast had one immortal and eight mortal heads for a total of nine heads. Heracles covered his mouth and nose to avoid the swamp's poison and attracted the hydra's attention by shooting flaming arrows near its lair. The beast charged out and attacked him, but Heracles managed to cut off several of its heads. However, the young hero soon realized that for every head he cut off, two more grew from the stumps. Heracles would have given in to hopelessness but he was not alone. His nephew, Iolaus (son of Heracles' twin brother) was with him, and the young man was loved and blessed by Athena. Her wisdom guided him in coming up with a plan. Iolaus followed behind Heracles with a torch and burned the stumps every time Heracles cut off one of the hydra's heads. His ploy worked and the monster began to falter.

But Hera was not done. She sent a giant crab into the fray. Heracles did not falter. With one stomp of his foot, he destroyed the creature. Finally, only the hydra's immortal head was left. Heracles cut this off with a golden sword gifted by Athena. Iolaus burnt the stump, and the hydra died. Knowing the blood of the hydra was poisonous, Heracles used it to coat the tip of his arrows.

Heracles was then ordered by his cousin to capture the Ceryneian Hind. This deer was both swift and beloved by Artemis. Its hooves were bronze while its antlers were gold. Heracles hunted the animal for a year before capturing it while it slept. Now Hera had intended for Artemis to punish Heracles in anger for daring to kidnap her beloved deer. However, when she and her twin, Apollo, appeared before Heracles, he begged her for forgiveness and explained his task and the purpose behind it. Artemis was moved and agreed to let him leave with the animal as long as he released it unharmed.

On Heracles' return, Eurystheus immediately tried to claim the sacred deer for himself. The young hero tricked his cousin into trying to lead the animal back to the palace. When Eurystheus tried to do so, Heracles released the animal and it ran back to the goddess.

"I am sorry, cousin," was Heracles' excuse, "you simply were not quick enough."

Eurystheus once again tried to orchestrate Heracles' death. This time, he sent him after the Erymanthian Boar. This boar was also sacred to Artemis. On his way to capture the boar, Heracles stopped by Pholus the centaur's dwelling, and shared a meal with him. Heracles had strong, undiluted wine with him and all the centaurs imbibed without watering it down. This made them so drunk they tried to attack and kill the hero. Heracles defended himself by shooting his poisoned arrows at them and the survivors fled to Chiron's cave. Heracles was so angry he pursued them, still shooting blindly. One of the arrows struck his dear mentor, Chiron.

As the first centaur, Chiron was immortal but the pain from the poison was unbearable. He begged Zeus to take his immortality and allow him to switch places with Prometheus. Zeus agreed. Heracles could not bear to witness his mentor being tormented by the eagle and used one of his poisoned arrows to kill it. Chiron then told Heracles how to capture the boar.

"Simply lure it into deep snow," the wise centaur advised him.

Heracles did so and captured the creature easily. When he brought it to his cousin, the terrified king hid and told Heracles to dispose of the boar.

After this had been done, Eurystheus gave Heracles his fifth task. Rather than simply trying to kill him, he sought to humiliate the hero. And so, he ordered him to clean King Augeas' stables in a single day. Augeas, king of Elis, had an enormous amount of healthy, beautiful, immortal horses. The dung they produced was plentiful, but the stables had not been mucked in three decades.

When he arrived at King Augeas' palace, Heracles asked for one-tenth of the king's cattle if he completed his task in the allotted time. The skeptical king agreed. Heracles immediately diverted two rivers and the stables were washed clean. Unfortunately, King Augeas refused to hold up his end of the deal. With the aid of Augeas' own son, Prince Peneus, Heracles took the deceitful king to court. The court ruled in Heracles' favor, and the angered, disgraced king banished the hero and his son from the kingdom before the court had even made its decision known. A furious Heracles immediately returned to Elis, slew the king, and put Peneus on the throne. Heracles then created the Olympic games to celebrate the completion of his task.

Heracles' next task was to slay the Stymphalian birds. These were monsters sacred to Ares with bronze beaks, metallic feathers, and poisonous dung. They were man-eaters who used their feathers to attack their prey. Heracles' attempts to reach them were hindered by the depth of the swamp they lived in. He knew that he would drown before he reached their lair. Once again, the goddess Athena came to her mortal half-brother's aid. She gave him a rattle that startled the birds and sent them flying. Once they were airborne, Heracles shot them down with his poisoned arrows. The surviving birds fled to distant lands.

Eurystheus then gave Heracles the seventh task. This time, the hero was required to capture the Cretan Bull. This beast had ravaged the island of Crete. With King Minos' permission, Heracles captured the bull using nothing but his hands and brought it back to his cousin. Eurystheus once again hid and ordered that the beast be given to Hera as a sacrifice. However, accepting this sacrifice would require Hera to acknowledge Heracles' successes so she refused. Heracles let the animal go and it wandered to another land where it was eventually caught and sacrificed to Artemis and Apollo by Theseus.

The eighth labor was capturing the Mares of Diomedes. Diomedes, King of Thrace, had raised his horses on human flesh. This drove them to madness and they developed the ability to breathe fire. Heracles realized he would not be able to complete the task alone and so he enlisted the help of several young men. They stole the animals but were chased by the Thracian army and had to flee. Heracles left the mares in the care of his friend, Abderus while he confronted the army. Unfortunately, the mares ate Abderus while Heracles was fighting Diomedes. The angered hero fed the king of Thrace to the mares and then built a city in his friend's memory. Eating their former master calmed the horses and Heracles bound their mouths. He brought them to Eurytheus who set the now peaceful mares free.

The next labor was influenced by Eurystheus' daughter, Admete. The princess desired the girdle Queen Hippolyta had been given by Ares. Eurystheus sent Heracles to obtain the girdle. On the way to the Amazons, two of Heracles' companions were slain by King Minos' son. Heracles killed the princes and took two of Minos' grandsons to replace his fallen comrades. He journeyed on to where the Amazons lived. Queen Hippolyta was in awe of the hero and readily agreed to give up the girdle, despite it being a gift from her father. However, Hera chose this moment to strike again. She spread a rumor among the Amazons that Heracles was trying to kidnap their queen. The warrior women took up arms against the hero and Heracles, thinking it was a plot by Hippolyta, killed her, took the girdle, and left.

The tenth labor would have been the final one if Eurystheus had not refused to acknowledge two of the tasks. The cowardly king ordered Heracles to steal the cattle of Geryon. To get to the cattle, Heracles had to cross the Libyan desert. The heat sapped his strength and so frustrated him that he shot an arrow at Helios, god of the sun. The god was taken by Heracles' bravery and offered him his golden chariot to ride. Heracles arrived at his destination in one night. To get to the cattle, Heracles first had to confront Orthrus, the two-headed brother of Cerberus. The hero killed the dog in one blow. He also killed the herdsman, Eurytion who attacked him after the dog was dead. Geryon was a giant with three human-like torsos connected by the waist. When he heard what the hero had done, he armed himself with three helmets, spears, and shields and confronted Heracles. One shot from Heracles' brow pierced his forehead and killed him instantly.

Bringing the cattle to Eurystheus was no easy task. Heracles slew two sons of Poseidon who tried to steal the cattle from him. One bull escaped into the sea and swam to Italy where he became a part of the king's herds. Heracles entrusted the care of the remaining cattle to the god Hephaestus and searched for the missing bull. When he found it, the ruler, Eryx, challenged him to a wrestling match. Heracles won three times in a row and killed the king.

After gathering all the cattle, Heracles faced the next challenge when Hera sent a gadfly to scatter the herd. Heracles once again had to bring them back together. The goddess then flooded a river and Heracles was forced to use stones to create a bridge. He finally drove the cattle to Eurystheus, where they were sacrificed.

It was at this point that Eurystheus announced that two of the labors were invalid.

"You had Iolaus help you with the hydra and you accepted payment for mucking King Augeas' stalls. The two rivers did the cleaning for you," the cowardly king declared.

So, Heracles found himself having to complete yet another task. This time, Eurystheus ordered him to steal three golden apples from the garden of the Hesperides. These nymphs were the daughters of Atlas and were associated with the sunset. Their garden was located far in the west. To obtain their precise location, Heracles grabbed hold of and wrestled with Nereus. Nereus was the son of Gaia. He was known as 'The Old Man of the Sea' and had the gift of prophecy and the ability to shapeshift. Heracles held on to Nereus despite the god shifting to all his forms. Eventually, the sea god relented and told Heracles what he wanted to know.

Heracles' journey was interrupted by Antaeus, the half-giant son of Gaia and Poseidon. During their fight, Heracles realized Antaeus drew strength from the earth and became invincible. The hero countered this by picking Antaeus off the ground and crushing him to death with his arms. After this Heracles finally found the garden. However, the garden was protected, and Heracles had difficulties retrieving the golden apples. He convinced Atlas to agree to a trade: Heracles would hold up the sky while Atlas fetched the apples. However, Atlas intended to betray the hero. The Titan decided he would leave Heracles with his burden and bring the apples to Eurystheus himself. Heracles pretended to agree to this but asked for one thing.

"If you would hold up the sky once again for just a few moments, I would like to adjust my cloak," he said.

Atlas agreed and once again shouldered the sky. But Heracles had no intention of staying. He retrieved the apples and went on his way.

And at last, Heracles had reached his final labor. Eurystheus charged him with capturing Cereberus, the three-headed dog guarded the Underworld. Heracles first had to learn the Eleusinian Mysteries, which taught him how to travel between the realms of the living and the dead. When he arrived at the entrance to Hades, the gods came to his aid. Athena and Hermes helped him enter the Underworld. Once there, Heracles wrestled Charon for safe passage across the Acheron river.

In the underworld, Heracles met Theseus and Pirithous who had been magically chained to chairs as punishment for trying to steal Persephone. He was able to save Theseus (though Theseus' thigh remained stuck to the chair) but could not save Pirithous (Hades refused to allow him to leave because he lusted after Persephone). Having rescued his cousin, the hero continued until he stood before Hades and requested that he be allowed to borrow Cereberus.

The god agreed. "However, you must take him yourself, without using any weapons."

The monstrous guard dog was no match for Heracles and soon found himself carried from the underworld to Eurystheus' palace. The cowardly king once again hid and ordered that Cereberus be returned to Hades. He also, finally, released Heracles from all his labors.

This was by no means the end of Heracles' adventures. He faced many trials, defeated men and monsters, and journeyed far and wide.

The Death of Heracles

Heracles eventually married a woman named Deianira. She was exquisitely beautiful, and the centaur, Nessus, tried to rape her. Heracles saved her by shooting the centaur with one of his poisoned arrows. With his dying breath, the centaur told her to mix his blood with olive oil and use it to keep her husband forever faithful to her. The naive Queen believed him and took his blood. Eventually, Heracles fell in love with another woman. Deianira remembered the centaur's words and mixed the blood with olive oil and smeared it on Heracles' shirt. She sent it to him, and he wore it. The hydra's toxin in Nessus' blood burned Heracles the second he donned the shirt. The pain was so incredible that he built a pyre, climbed on top of it, and begged those around him to light it. A passerby did so in exchange for his bow and arrows. Heracles died and ascended to Olympus as a god.

Chapter 6: Theseus

The Six Labors of Theseus

Despite having two wives, Aegeus, king of Athens, found himself without an heir. As men did at that time, he journeyed to the Oracle of Delphi for guidance. However, the prophecy they gave him was cryptic. King Aegeus reached out to Pittheus, king of Troezen, for help. The cunning king understood the prophecy immediately and schemed to have his daughter, Aethra, sleep with Aegeus. However, Poseidon also slept with the princess that very same night. She soon became pregnant. King Aegeus decided to return home but warned her not to tell the child of his heritage.

"If the child is a boy, show him this rock where I will leave my gifts. If he can retrieve them, send him to me so I will know he is the heir to my kingdom."

Whether he was the son of King Aegeus or Poseidon himself, Theseus grew to be a man of bravery and power. His adventures began when he reached manhood. On that day, his mother showed him the stone Aegeus had left.

"Under this stone," she said, "are gifts from your father. If you are strong enough to lift it and retrieve these gifts, you may journey to be with him."

Theseus eagerly lifted the stone and discovered the sandals and sword hidden underneath. Seeing he was old and strong enough, his mother advised him to turn over the items to King Aegeus of Athens.

"If you do this, you will learn about your father," she told him.

Theseus immediately set out on his quest. However, the journey was not as simple as he had anticipated. His path brought him to the dwelling grounds of Periphetes, son of Hephaestus. One of his legs was lame and he only had one eye. Despite this, he attacked and savagely beat any traveler who crossed his path. He would then take all their possessions for himself. Unfortunately for the bandit, when he tried to kill Theseus with his bronze club, the hero wrestled it from him and clubbed him to death. Theseus then kept the club for himself.

As his travels continued, Theseus met another robber, Sinis. Known as the Pine-Bender, Sinis would tie a man between two bent pine trees and then release them. When the pine trees sprang back to their original position the man would be brutally torn in two. Theseus quickly overcame him and treated him to the same fate as those he had killed. The hero went even further and slept with and impregnated Sinis' daughter.

Theseus went to the land of Crommyon, where he encountered the Crommyonian Sow. The wild sow had terrorized the land and Theseus killed her. After this, Theseus met yet another robber, Sciron. Sciron was known for making travelers wash his feet. When they bent down to do so, he would kick them off the cliff and into the sea where they were devoured by the giant turtle waiting hungrily at the bottom. Once again, Theseus meted out poetic justice. As Sciron was getting ready to kick him, Theseus grabbed the robber and threw him off the cliff. The turtle did not hesitate in eating him.

When Theseus arrived in Eleusis, he met King Cercyon. The King was known for challenging travelers to a wrestling match to the death. However, Theseus was more skilled than the king and threw him to the ground so hard that he died. Once again, Theseus slept with the daughter of the man he had killed.

The final obstacle Theseus encountered before arriving in Athens was Procrustes. Now, Procrustes seemed like a kind and hospitable man. Whenever a traveler passed by, he would offer them a bed to spend the night. However, any traveler who accepted and laid down was soon made by Procrustes to fit the bed. He cut their legs off with an axe if they were too tall or elongated them by hammering their legs if they were too short. As with the others, Theseus overcame him. And though Procrustes fit the bed perfectly, the hero cut off his legs and head.

After his long and troubled journey, the young prince finally arrived in Athens. However, by this time, Aegeus had remarried the enchantress Medea. She quickly recognized Theseus and saw him as a threat to her son who she considered the future king of Athens. Medea had already proven she was ruthless and bloodthirsty by murdering her two children by the hero, Jason, in revenge for him leaving her for another woman. She convinced Aegeus that this strange young man was a danger to him and convinced the king to send him after the Marathonian Bull. This bull had formerly been known as the Cretan Bull, which Heracles had captured as one of his labors. Like his cousin, Theseus managed to hunt and capture the animal. He brought it before Aegeus and Medea before sacrificing it to the twin gods Artemis and Apollo.

But Medea was not deterred. She then tried to poison the young prince during a feast. Luckily, King Aegeus recognized his sandals and sword and guessed his wife's intention. The King immediately knocked the wine from his son's hands and banished Medea. Aegeus welcomed his son and named him the heir to Athens' throne.

Theseus and the Minotaur

Theseus had not been in Athens for long before he discovered the tribute they were forced to pay King Minos of Crete. Every year, seven maidens and seven warriors were sent to the labyrinth in Crete where they were devoured by the Minotaur. The Cretan king had imposed this tax as punishment for the murder of his sons by the Athenians.

Now, this Minotaur was the product of King Minos' wife, Pasiphae, and the Cretan Bull. The Queen had been cursed to lust after the bull and had slept with it in secret. The result was a child with a human body and a man's head. An embarrassed Minos had commissioned the great inventor Daedalus to build a labyrinth to store the Minotaur.

After hearing about the tribute, Theseus begged his father to allow him to be among the warriors chosen for sacrifice. "I will kill the Minotaur and free our people."

Aegeus agreed on one condition.

"Promise me that if you leave to return, you will fly white sails on your ship," the king said. "That way I will see the ships sailing back from a distance and know my precious son is alive."

Theseus agreed and set off with the rest of the tributes. When they arrived in Crete, he boldly declared to King Minos that he would kill the monster in the labyrinth. Minos met his claims with derision. However, Theseus' bravery and noble bearing caught the attention of Princess Ariadne. She fell deeply in love with him and resolved to help him with his quest. The princess begged Daedalus to tell her the secret to navigating the labyrinth.

The inventor did so and gave her a ball of thread which she gave to Theseus.

"Let this unravel as you go through the labyrinth. It will help you find your way back out," she told the young hero.

Theseus accepted the thread and plunged deep into the depths of the labyrinth. He found the Minotaur at the center and slew him after a brief battle. The hero then left the labyrinth by following the thread. He took the princess, gathered his men, and fled. As promised in exchange for her help, Theseus married Ariadne during one of their brief stops on an island.

But Theseus' and Ariadne's marriage was fated to end as quickly as their love had begun. While the princess was still sleeping, Theseus and his men boarded their ship and left her behind. She woke up alone and was devastated. However, the god, Dionysus, had fallen in love with her and came to her rescue. He made her his wife and took her to Olympus to live with him.

Theseus, meanwhile, continued sailing home. In all the excitement he forgot his promise to his father. The grieving king saw the black sails on the ship and threw himself to his death. What would have been a joyous homecoming for Theseus turned into one of grief. The young hero was crowned king in his father's stead.

The Death of Theseus

While Theseus was a great king who accomplished many things, his choice of friends and interactions with women eventually led to his undoing. He became friends with King Pirithous and both journeyed to the Amazons to capture wives. Theseus' wife bore him a son called Hippolytus. However, Theseus grew tired of her and married Ariadne's sister, Phaedra, instead. Phaedra fell in love with Hippolytus, but he spurned her. In revenge, she told Theseus that his son had raped her. An angry Theseus cursed his son, and Hippolytus ended up being killed by his horses. Phaedra hung herself.

Theseus began looking for another wife. Pirithous and Theseus decided that as children of gods they deserved to marry daughters of gods. Theseus chose the young Helen of Troy and kidnapped her. He gave the child to his mother to raise until she was of marrying age, but Helen's brother rescued her. Despite the loss of Helen, Theseus agreed to journey to the underworld to capture Persephone so Pirithous could marry her. They failed and were punished for their crime.

Theseus remained in the underworld for many years before he was freed by Heracles. He returned to Athens to find that a new ruler had been selected. This ruler was disinclined to give up his throne, so Theseus fled to Scyros, where King Lycomedes welcomed him. But Lycomedes was a supporter of Athens' new ruler. While pretending to give Theseus a tour of the island, Lycomedes pushed the hero off a cliff.

Conclusion

Greek mythology was more than just stories to the Ancient Greeks. They were roadmaps that taught them how to live and how to worship. It formed their religion, directed their lives, and helped them to understand the world around them. The Greeks were not prone to stuffy religious texts. They welcomed storytellers who added to their understanding of the gods.

The Greeks believed in many gods. Of the hundreds that they worshipped, fourteen stood as the main cornerstone of their religion. Twelve of these were known as the Olympians, led by Zeus, the god of thunder and justice. These gods were not perfect. They were violent, lustful, capricious, and cruel. They meddled in the affairs of men, slept with countless women, and populated the earth with demigods and monsters. The Greeks believed that dishonoring the gods or not honoring them enough led to horrible consequences.

In addition to the gods, the Greeks had many stories about heroes. These heroes were often children of the gods and performed great deeds. They were held as examples of being a strong and courageous human. However, many of these heroes suffered tragic fates due to their pride and disrespect for the gods. The Greeks learned as much from the heroes' flaws as they did from their accomplishments.

Today, Greek mythology is prevalent in modern society. It can be seen in medicine, philosophy, astrology, and language. The stories have been retold in countless ways. The intricate and beautiful stories of Greek mythology shine a light on the mindset of an ancient people while capturing the imagination of present society.

References

Adkins, A. & Pollard, J.R.T. (2020). Greek religion. Encyclopedia Britannica. https://www.britannica.com/topic/Greek-religion

Ancient Greek myth for kids: The gift of fire - Zeus & Prometheus - Ancient Greek myth for kids (n.d.) https://greece.mrdonn.org/greekgods/prometheus.html

Aphrodite (2014). Greek Gods & Goddesses. https://greekgodsandgoddesses.net/goddesses/aphrodite/

Apollo (2014). Greek Gods & Goddesses. https://greekgodsandgoddesses.net/gods/apollo/

Ares (2014) Greek Gods & Goddesses. https://greekgodsandgoddesses.net/gods/ares/

Artemis (2014). Greek Gods & Goddesses. https://greekgodsandgoddesses.net/goddesses/artemis/

Athena (2014) Greek Gods & Goddesses. https://greekgodsandgoddesses.net/goddesses/athena/

Atsma, A.J. (n.d.) Chiron (Kheiron) – elder centaur of Greek Mythology. https://www.theoi.com/Georgikos/KentaurosKheiron.html

Atsma, A.J. (n.d.) Pasiphae- Greek goddess and witch – queen of Crete. https://www.theoi.com/Titan/Pasiphae.html

Atsma, A.J. (n.d.). CHARON (Kharon) - ferryman of the dead, underworld daemon of Greek mythology https://www.theoi.com/Khthonios/Kharon.html

Atsma, A.J. (n.d.). Echidna (Ekhidna) – serpent-nymph mother of monsters in Greek mythology. https://www.theoi.com/Ther/DrakainaEkhidna1.html

Britannica, T. Editors of Encyclopaedia (2007). Aeacus. Encyclopedia Britannica. https://www.britannica.com/topic/Aeacus

Britannica, T. Editors of Encyclopaedia (2019). Hephaestus. Encyclopedia Britannica. https://www.britannica.com/topic/Hephaestus

Britannica, T. Editors of Encyclopaedia (2020). Aphrodite. Encyclopedia Britannica. https://www.britannica.com/topic/Aphrodite-Greek-mythology

Britannica, T. Editors of Encyclopaedia (2020). Demeter. Encyclopedia Britannica. https://www.britannica.com/topic/Demeter

Britannica, T. Editors of Encyclopaedia (2020). Hera. Encyclopedia Britannica. https://www.britannica.com/topic/Hera

Britannica, T. Editors of Encyclopaedia (2020). Theseus. Encyclopedia Britannica. https://www.britannica.com/topic/Theseus-Greek-hero

Britannica, T. Editors of Encyclopaedia (2021). Athena. Encyclopedia Britannica. https://www.britannica.com/topic/Athena-Greek-mythology

Britannica, T. Editors of Encyclopaedia (2021). Hades. Encyclopedia Britannica. https://www.britannica.com/topic/Hades-Greek-mythology

Britannica, T. Editors of Encyclopaedia (2021). Heracles. Encyclopedia Britannica. https://www.britannica.com/topic/Heracles

Britannica, T. Editors of Encyclopaedia (2021). Hestia. Encyclopedia Britannica. https://www.britannica.com/topic/Hestia

Britannica, T. Editors of Encyclopaedia (2021). Odysseus. Encyclopedia Britannica. https://www.britannica.com/topic/Odysseus

Britannica, T. Editors of Encyclopaedia (2021). Poseidon. Encyclopedia Britannica. https://www.britannica.com/topic/Poseidon

Britannica, T. Editors of Encyclopaedia (2021). Prometheus. Encyclopedia Britannica. https://www.britannica.com/topic/Prometheus-Greek-god

Britannica, T. Editors of Encyclopaedia (2021). Typhon. Encyclopedia Britannica. https://www.britannica.com/topic/Typhon

Britannica, T. Editors of Encyclopaedia (2021). Zeus. Encyclopedia Britannica. https://www.britannica.com/topic/Zeus

Cartwright, M. (2012). Achilles. World History Encyclopedia. https://www.worldhistory.org/achilles/

Cartwright, M. (2012). Perseus. World History Encyclopedia. https://www.worldhistory.org/Perseus/

Cartwright, M. (2016). Theseus. World History Encyclopedia. https://www.worldhistory.org/Theseus/

Cartwright, M. (2018). Ancient Greek religion. World History Encyclopedia. https://www.worldhistory.org/Greek_Religion/

Demeter (2014). Greek Gods and Goddesses. https://greekgodsandgoddesses.net/goddesses/demeter/

Dionysus (2014). Greek Gods and Goddesses. https://greekgodsandgoddesses.net/gods/dionysus/

Echidna, (2017). Greek Gods & Goddesses. https://greekgodsandgoddesses.net/myths/echidna/

Gill, N.S. (2021). Hesiod's Five Ages of Man. https://www.thoughtco.com/the-five-ages-of-man-111776

GreekBoston.com (n.d.). What are the six labors of Theseus https://www.greekboston.com/culture/mythology/six-labors-theseus/

GreekMythology.com, T. Editors of Website (2015). Hector. GreekMythology.com Website. https://www.greekmythology.com/Myths/Mortals/Hector/hector.html

GreekMythology.com, T. Editors of Website (2021) Perseus. GreekMythology.com Website. https://www.greekmythology.com/Myths/Heroes/Perseus/perseus.html

GreekMythology.com, T. Editors of Website (2021). Aeacus. GreekMythology.com Website. https://www.greekmythology.com/Myths/Mortals/Aeacus/aeacus.html

GreekMythology.com, T. Editors of Website (2021). Aphrodite. GreekMythology.com Website. https://www.greekmythology.com/Olympians/Aphrodite/aphrodite.html

GreekMythology.com, T. Editors of Website (2021). Apollo. GreekMythology.com Website. https://www.greekmythology.com/Olympians/Apollo/apollo.html

GreekMythology.com, T. Editors of Website (2021). Ares. GreekMythology.com Website. https://www.greekmythology.com/Olympians/Aris/aris.html

GreekMythology.com, T. Editors of Website (2021). Artemis. GreekMythology.com Website. https://www.greekmythology.com/Olympians/Artemis/artemis.html

GreekMythology.com, T. Editors of Website (2021). Athena. GreekMythology.com Website. https://www.greekmythology.com/Olympians/Athena/athena.html

GreekMythology.com, T. Editors of Website (2021). Demeter. GreekMythology.com Website. https://www.greekmythology.com/Other_Gods/Demeter/demeter.html

GreekMythology.com, T. Editors of Website (2021). Dionysus. GreekMythology.com Website.

https://www.greekmythology.com/Other_Gods/Dionysus/dionysus.html

GreekMythology.com, T. Editors of Website (2021). Hades. GreekMythology.com Website. https://www.greekmythology.com/Olympians/Hades/hades.html

GreekMythology.com, T. Editors of Website (2021). Hephaestus. GreekMythology.com Website. https://www.greekmythology.com/Olympians/Hephaestus/hephaestus.html

GreekMythology.com, T. Editors of Website (2021). Hera. GreekMythology.com Website. https://www.greekmythology.com/Olympians/Hera/hera.html

GreekMythology.com, T. Editors of Website (2021). Heracles. GreekMythology.com Website. https://www.greekmythology.com/Myths/Heroes/Heracles/heracles.html

GreekMythology.com, T. Editors of Website (2021). Hermes. GreekMythology.com Website. https://www.greekmythology.com/Olympians/Hermes/hermes.html

GreekMythology.com, T. Editors of Website (2021). Hestia. GreekMythology.com Website. https://www.greekmythology.com/Olympians/Hestia/hestia.html

GreekMythology.com, T. Editors of Website (2021). Jason. GreekMythology.com Website. https://www.greekmythology.com/Myths/Heroes/Jason/jason.html

GreekMythology.com, T. Editors of Website (2021). Labours of Heracles. GreekMythology.com Website. https://www.greekmythology.com/Myths/The_Myths/L abours_of_Heracles/labours_of_heracles.html

GreekMythology.com, T. Editors of Website (2021). Orpheus. GreekMythology.com Website. https://www.greekmythology.com/Myths/Mortals/Orph eus/orpheus.html

GreekMythology.com, T. Editors of Website (2021). Perseus. GreekMythology.com Website. https://www.greekmythology.com/Myths/Heroes/Perse us/perseus.html

GreekMythology.com, T. Editors of Website (2021). Poseidon. GreekMythology.com Website. https://www.greekmythology.com/Olympians/Poseidon /poseidon.html

GreekMythology.com, T. Editors of Website (2021). Sirens. GreekMythology.com Website. https://www.greekmythology.com/Myths/Creatures/Sir ens/sirens.html

GreekMythology.com, T. Editors of Website (2021). The Creation. GreekMythology.com Website. https://www.greekmythology.com/Myths/The_Myths/T he_Creation/the_creation.html

GreekMythology.com, T. Editors of Website (2021). Theseus. GreekMythology.com Website. https://www.greekmythology.com/Myths/Heroes/These us/theseus.html

GreekMythology.com, T. Editors of Website (2021). Zeus. GreekMythology.com Website.

https://www.greekmythology.com/Olympians/Zeus/zeus.html

Hades (2014) Greek Gods & Goddesses. https://greekgodsandgoddesses.net/gods/hades/

Hephaestus (2014). Greek Gods & Goddesses. https://greekgodsandgoddesses.net/gods/hephaestus/

Heracles (2020). Livius. https://www.livius.org/articles/mythology/heracles/

Heracles in Greek Mythology (n.d.) https://www.greeklegendsandmyths.com/heracles.html

Hermes (2014). Greek Gods & Goddesses. https://greekgodsandgoddesses.net/gods/hermes/

Hestia (2014) Greek Gods & Goddesses. https://greekgodsandgoddesses.net/goddesses/hestia/

History.com Editors (2009). Greek mythology. https://www.history.com/topics/ancient-history/greek-mythology

Hunt, J.M. (n.d.) https://www.desy.de/gna/interpedia/greek_myth/creation.html#:~:text=From%20Love%20came%20Light%20and,to%20man%20out%20of%20darkness

Madeleine (2019). Jason Greek: Who is Jason in Greek mythology. https://www.theoi.com/articles/jason-greek-who-is-jason-in-greek-mythology/

Myth of Perseus and Andromeda - Greek myths (n.d.) https://www.greeka.com/greece-myths/perseus-andromeda/

Myth of Theseus, the legendary king of Athens (n.d.). https://www.greeka.com/attica/athens/myths/theseus/

Pandora's box, the Greek myth of Pandora and her box (n.d.) https://www.greekmyths-greekmythology.com/pandoras-box-myth/

Poseidon (2014). Greek Gods & Goddesses. https://greekgodsandgoddesses.net/gods/poseidon/

Quartermain, C. (2019). Suitors of Helen in Greek mythology. https://owlcation.com/humanities/Suitors-of-Helen#:~:text=Other%20notable%20names%20that%20appear,brother%20to%20Ajax%20the%20Great

The creation of the Milky Way in Greek mythology (n.d.) https://www.greeklegendsandmyths.com/the-milky-way.html

The Greek gods: Full list and background (2020). https://greektraveltellers.com/blog/the-greek-gods

The labors of Theseus (2020). https://www.greeklegendsandmyths.com/labours-of-theseus.html

The myth of Theseus and the Minotaur (n.d.) https://www.greekmyths-greekmythology.com/myth-of-theseus-and-minotaur/

The Sirens in Greek mythology (n.d.) https://www.greeklegendsandmyths.com/the-sirens.html

Theseus and the Minotaur- Greek mythology (n.d.) https://sites.google.com/site/basicgreekmythology/hero-s/theseus/theseus-and-the-marathonian-bull

Typhon-the father of all monsters (2017). Greek Gods and Goddesses.
https://greekgodsandgoddesses.net/gods/typhon/

www.ingramcontent.com/pod-product-compliance
Lightning Source LLC
Chambersburg PA
CBHW070938120626
46546CB00004B/1461